New Zealand Today

New Zealand Today

Eleanor Z. Baker

Steck-Vaughn Company
An Intext Publisher
Austin, Texas

Library of Congress Cataloging in Publication Data
Baker, Eleanor Z
    New Zealand today.
SUMMARY: Describes the geography, history, flora and
fauna, government, economy, culture, and people of the
country lying halfway between the equator and the South
Pole.
    1. New Zealand—Juvenile literature. [1. New Zealand]
I. Title.
DU412.B325   919.31   72-640
ISBN 0-8114-7746-0
                    ISBN 0-8114-7746-0
        Library of Congress Catalog Card Number 72-640
Copyright © 1972 by Steck-Vaughn Company, Austin, Texas
                    All Rights Reserved
        Printed and Bound in the United States of America

Dedicated with love and pride to my daughter,
Susan Ellen Baker,
on the occasion of her high school graduation

Acknowledgments

The photographs used in this book have been generously contributed by The High Commissioner for New Zealand through the Office of the Photo Library, London.

Statistical figures and reference information were made available through the offices of the New Zealand Information Service, Tourist and Publicity Department, Wellington, New Zealand.

Eleanor Z. Baker

New Zealand

Map showing land use in New Zealand. At one time 70% of the land was forest. This figure has been reduced to about 23% today. The Kaingora State Forest on North Island is the largest planted forest in the world. Forestry is increasing in significance in land use in New Zealand.

Tasman Sea

NORTH AUCKLAND

Auckland

Bay of Plenty

Coromandel Peninsula

AUCKLAND

Rotorua

GISBORNE

TARANAKI

HAWKES BAY

Wanganui

WELLINGTON

Wellington

Cook Strait

NELSON

MARLBOROUGH

WESTLAND

Christchurch

South Pacific Ocean

CANTERBURY

OTAGO

Milford Sound

Dunedin

SOUTHLAND

STEWART ISLAND

Sheep farming (wool and store)

Intensive sheep farming (fat lamb)

Intensive sheep farming with cash cropping

Dairying and fat lamb farming

Orchards and market farming

Introduction

What country lies halfway between the equator and the South Pole? Nestled securely in the vivid blue waters of the Pacific Ocean, the country is New Zealand. But unless viewed from close range, the land appears to be hidden from view because of the curvature of the earth.

New Zealand is a green land distinguished by great forests of towering trees. The forests shield giant ferns and some of the most primitive forms of animal life in the world. Many species of both vegetation and animals are endemic, meaning that they are not seen in any other part of the world. These endemic forms include bats, birds, lizards, and plants.

The native Polynesian people, the Maoris, are strong and proud. They resisted the coming of the *Pakeha*, or white man, for a long time, but now both peoples work together for the progress of their country.

Maoris recall their achievements in the art of war in song and dance. The quick tempo of their music and the fierceness of their expressions reflect an ever-present vitality and courageous spirit.

> The north is warm.
> The south is cold.
> The best-known native birds cannot fly.
> It is a land of contrasts.
> It is *New Zealand today.*

New Zealand's History

When New Zealand was discovered by a Dutch navigator, Abel Tasman, in 1642, the land was inhabited by the Maoris (*Mow*-uh-rees). Many years later, in 1769, Captain James Cook of England made the first of several visits to the new land. On the first visit, he mapped the two main islands, North Island and South Island, and the passage between them, Cook Strait, which is named after him.

Organized colonization by the British didn't begin until 1840. Settling was a dangerous occupation, as the Maoris tried to keep the white man out of their land. Most of the fighting took place in the north, but by the end of the 1800s, the Maori and the Pakeha (Paa-*kee*-haa) had reconciled their differences and were living peacefully together.

In 1852 Britain granted self-government to New Zealand, and the New Zealand Constitutional Act of the same year made no distinction between the two peoples as to the granting of political rights. Thus, from the beginning of constitutional government in New Zealand, the Maori has had political rights. Today, New Zealand is an independent empire of the British Commonwealth, and the bond between the people of New Zealand and Great Britain is strong.

New Zealand's Geography

New Zealand is in the Southern Hemisphere, approximately 1,000 miles in length from north to south. In area, New Zealand has over 103,000 square miles and is about two-thirds the size of the state of California. A smaller island—Stewart Island—is located south of South Island. Many small islands, both populated and unpopulated, lie around the coast. The unique geographical features of New Zealand can be explained by the fact that the country is geographically young, characterized by rolling, hilly country with a chain of mountains running down the center of both North Island and South Island. Three-fourths of the country is 650 feet or more above sea level, and there are numerous mountain peaks above 7,500 feet. The mountains of South Island are the most spectacular and are called the "Southern Alps." The most famous mountain summit in New Zealand is Mount Cook on South Island, rising majestically to 12,349 feet amidst glaciers and other peaks which are snow covered throughout the year.

Because New Zealand is mountainous and almost all of the rivers are short and torrential, most rivers run swiftly to the sea. No part of New Zealand is more than eighty miles from the seacoast. The country is quite narrow in comparison with its length, and although the coastline has few natural harbors, there are many attractive beaches.

Left: A view of the Wanganui River on North Island.

Right: Fox Glacier, South Island, Westland Province, showing Victoria Range, Chancellor Ridge, Pioneer Ridge, and Douglas Peak.

The highest peaks of the Southern Alps are seen reflected in the calm waters of Lake Matheson. Mount Tasman is on the left, and Mount Cook is on the right. This view is from South Island, Westland Province.

3

Left: Bridal Veil Falls at Te Mata, Auckland Province, North Island.

Right: Mitre Peak in Milford Sound, South Island.

Much of the land of New Zealand has been utilized for the creation of national parks. These beautiful areas are preserved as far as possible in their natural state.

Since New Zealand lies in the Southern Hemisphere, summer comes in December, and winter begins in June. Surprisingly enough, however, the range of temperature throughout the year is quite small due to the narrow width of the land and the fact that it is surrounded by water. Therefore, the climate is fairly mild, having

4

an average temperature of 56° Fahrenheit in North Island and 51° Fahrenheit in South Island. Bright sunshine averages between 1700 and 2000 hours annually, and there is a regular distribution of rainfall through the four seasons. These factors make it possible for cows, sheep, and other stock to graze all year in most areas.

New Zealand lies within a vast belt of volcanoes and earthquake faults that run from the Antarctic through New Zealand and the South Pacific islands up through the Philippines to Japan, across the Aleutians and south along the west coast of North America through the states of Washington, Oregon, and California, and then along the western coast of South America to Tierra del Fuego.

Australia is not included in this "rim of fire" that borders the Pacific Ocean, but the effects of this belt are frequently felt in New Zealand. Active volcanoes on the North Island include Ruapehu (Roo-uh-*pe*-hoo) 9,175 feet, Ngauruhoe (Ngaa-oo-roo-haw-*e*) 7,515 feet, and Tongariro (Tawn-guh-*ree*-raw) 6,548 feet. These three volcanoes are mildly active but are located far from any large centers of population. The southern part of North Island and the northern part of South Island are subject to earthquakes which are, fortunately, seldom destructive.

Left: The moa. No one has left a written record or a drawing of a moa—the large, flightless relative of the Kiwis. However, artists have reconstructed images of the birds from skeletal remains.

Right: The tuatara is New Zealand's unique living fossil, the only survivor of an order of reptiles that lived millions of years ago. Once found in many parts of New Zealand, the tuatara lives only on a few coastal islands, usually sharing the burrow of the petrel, a small sea bird.

New Zealand's Animals

Although New Zealand is regarded as a young land geologically, there is evidence that this land lay remote and primeval for millions of years, unknown to man and almost unknown by any other form of life. During this early period, there were no land animals except birds, bats, lizards, and the *tuatara* (too-uh-*tar*-uh). The tuatara is the sole survivor of an extinct order of reptiles which still retain vestiges of the pineal, or third, eye possessed by prehistoric animals. This lizardlike reptile is the only survivor from the age of giant reptiles, the brontosaurs and dinosaurs. The tuatara, a "living fossil," is found now only on some of the scattered islands off New Zealand.

New Zealand's Birds

Two of New Zealand's best-known birds, the *moa* (*mah*-uh) and the *kiwi* (*kee*-wee), had so little use for their wings that they gradually lost all but a trace of them. The huge wingless moa is now extinct, but it once was the world's largest bird.

Many scientists believe that it was the moa which played the greatest part in the early development of the country, for the early inhabitants have been called "moa hunters." There were about twenty-two species of moa in New Zealand, with the largest birds averaging eight and one-half feet in height and the smallest about the size of a large turkey. Archaeological finds have established the existence of the moa as far back as fifteen-million years ago. The smallest species of the moa became extinct in the North Islands more than a hundred years ago. In the South Islands, moa bones, feathers, and eggs are sometimes found in remote caves. Not only was the flesh eaten, but moa feathers were used for decoration. The bones were used for tools or ornaments, and the eggs, especially those of the larger species—which might measure up to ten inches by seven inches—were used as water bottles. The moa was to the native peoples what the buffalo was to the Plains Indians of North America.

Left: The tui, one of the famed songbirds of New Zealand. Golden cascades of the kowhai tree attract the birds in spring.

Right: A South Island Kiwi leaving its burrow at nightfall to feed in the dense forest. This flightless bird is native to New Zealand.

A distant relative of the moa, the flightless kiwi, is still a popular symbol of New Zealand today. In fact, New Zealanders refer to themselves as "Kiwis." The kiwi has a long sensitive beak with nostrils at the end to ferret out worms and insects. The bird has reddish-brown plumage and is slightly larger in size than a chicken. Speed in running compensates for the loss of flight. In proportion to its size, the kiwi's egg is unusually large.

Another ground bird, the *takahe* (*taa*-kaa-eh), believed extinct for half a century, was rediscovered in 1948 in a remote valley of South Island. The takahe is now protected by the government's declaration of the bird's natural habitat as a closed sanctuary.

Other well-known birds of New Zealand, the *tui* (*too*-ee) and the *bellbird,* are famed songsters. The bold and beautiful tui normally lives in the forest but has learned to live with human neighbors and visits public and private gardens, especially when nectar-blooming flowers and shrubs are in bloom. The tui is a well-known mimic,

and Maoris often pay a compliment to a speaker by saying "He has the throat of a tui." Shyer than the tui is the bellbird, whose sweet voice sounds like the soft melodious chime of bells. Like the tui, bellbirds are found throughout New Zealand.

The distinctive "more-pork" cry is one of the most characteristic night sounds of New Zealand. The cry belongs to the New Zealand night owl, the *morepork*. The owls are active at night and relish mice for their dinner.

The thousands of miles of New Zealand coastline are a perfect setting for sea and water birds of many species. Some of the most amusing coastal birds are the penguins. They are distinguished by their tuxedo-dress appearance. These unusual looking creatures divide their time between the sea and shore, using their shore stay for breeding. Among species found in New Zealand are the foot-tall Little Blue Penguin, the Crested Penguin, and the Yellow-Eyed Penguin.

New Zealand's Plants

Dark green, light green, glossy green, perhaps a dash of white or red or yellow—this is the New Zealand forest. It is tropical in appearance without the tropical riot of colors found in many other lands. The predominance of the green color is highlighted by the occasional appearance of native flowers. The majority of these luxuriant flowers are white or green in color.

A well-known spring flower is the clematis vine that features masses of white, starry blossoms which twine in and out of the tree-tops. It was named "puawananga" (poo-uh-*waa*-nang-uh), meaning sanctified flower, by the Maoris. The *kowhai* (*kaw*-whaa-ee) is generally regarded as the unofficial national flower and blossoms into golden cascades on the kowhai tree. The hanging flowers have petals that resemble pea pods, and, unlike the few native trees in New Zealand, the kowhai tends to lose its leaves during the winter. The "Christmas tree," or *pohutukawa* (*paw*-hoo-too-kuh-wuh), is a tree that is mainly found on the northern coast. The profusion of crimson blossoms that appear in December are a unique Christmas present for New Zealanders.

On South Island, amid towering mountain ranges, New Zealand boasts a spectacular display of alpine flowers. The most common and best known of these flowers are the white or yellow mountain daisies of which there are at least sixty varieties, and the mountain lily native to the lower slopes of the New Zealand Southern Alps range. The mountain lily may bear as many as fifty sparkling white blossoms at a time and is considered to be one of the most beautiful plants in the world. The most valuable plant is New Zealand flax which features tough, dark green leaves that often grow to more

Kowhai

Pohutukawa

Pauwananga

Mountain Daisies

than six feet in length. From the leaves the native Maoris once
made nets, baskets, mats, robes, and capes. Sometimes they dyed
the fibers so they could weave geometric patterns. Since the early
days of New Zealand's trading history, flax fiber has been exported
for the making of rope. The fiber is also considered valuable for
the production of soft linenlike fabric.

Right: A traditional Maori dance using poi (paw-ee) balls. The woven design of the women's bodices is called "taniko" (taa-nee-kaw).

Below: Traditional Maori dress. Decorative feathers used on the cloak were taken from the kiwi and the *huia* (hoo-ee-uh), a bird that is now extinct.

A demonstration of the traditional challenge of the Maori warrior. Such gestures were made to determine if visitors to a Maori village came in war or peace and to intimidate any aggressors.

New Zealand's Aborigines

The aborigines (ab-uh-*rij*-uh-nees), or people living in New Zealand when it was discovered, are called "Maoris," and they are Polynesian (Pol-uh-*nee*-shun) in origin. The word "Polynesia" means *many islands*. The great expedition which is regarded as the major date of settlement in New Zealand took place in the fourteenth century. The voyagers landed on North Island of New Zealand. Finding the land suitable for their way of life, they remained there, although a few tribes settled later on South Island.

The Maoris divided into tribes on the basis of kinship to a common ancestor, making all the member of each tribe related to one

another—although frequently this relationship was quite distant. Members could marry within the tribe provided the relationships were more distant than that of first cousins. While groups existed within the tribe, the tribal community itself was most important. To a larger degree than most native peoples, the Maoris encouraged a high degree of participation in community activities. In a very real sense, the community became the family unit for most Maoris.

The villages of the Maoris were protected by a fort or some other defended position called a "pa." Fighting was frequent, and men were trained in the use of short-handled and long-handled clubs. The Maoris liked to fight and were unusually proficient in the art— as the Europeans were to learn the hard way when they settled in New Zealand. Fighting and killing were accompanied by cannibalism, the practice of cooking and eating one's victims. Particularly appealing was the body of a powerful warrior killed in battle or ambush. It was thought that the eating of such a warrior's flesh would make the consumers better warriors.

The Maoris were, of necessity, farmers; and whenever possible, large-scale attacks took place at a time when food was plentiful or after the fields were planted or crops were harvested. Crops of the enemy were often destroyed, for depriving a tribe of food during the winter period was a severe blow.

Like other Polynesian peoples of the South Pacific, the Maoris were artistic. While they were most skilled in carving, they were also impressive in their performance of music and the dance. The music was quite unusual, for their ancient chants were limited to musical sounds all within the limits of three musical tones as we know them. The entire range of these songs might go from "do" to "mi" on a regular scale. They also used several tones in between these notes to give variety to their music. Most of the instruments were either shell trumpets or flutes made of bone, stone, or wood. Ceremonial dancing was always important in Maori life, and, like the music, combined harmony and rhythm. Even today, visitors

14

are impressed by the fierce *haka* (*huh*-kaa) which is performed solely by men who accompany it with terrifying expressions and the brandishing of weapons.

Ceremony and ritual were important to almost every phase of Maori life. All Maoris were careful to observe the laws of *tapu* (*taa*-poo), or taboo, which defined the manner in which burial grounds, homes, and storehouses should be protected. Anyone who broke a law of tapu might suffer death through the practice of black magic by the Maori priests. The priests were men who were thought to have a command of telepathy, or "second sight," and other supernatural powers. Their curse was sufficient to sometimes cause an offender to die from fear alone.

The Maoris were a religious people. Their religion was characterized by belief in a supreme being called "Io" (Ee-aw). But most of the people were more familiar with the lesser gods who were in charge of every phase of their lives. These gods included *Tu* (Too), the god of war; *Rongo* (Rawn-gaw), the protector of crops; and *Tangaroa* (Tuh-nguh-*raw*-uh), the god of the sea. Maoris believed that after death their souls took flight for a cloudlike homeland far to the north. In this afterlife they remained forever, following the same interests they had had on earth. There was no idea of a heaven for the good or punishment for evildoers.

English missionaries arrived in the early 1800s with little knowledge or understanding about Maori practices and tried to convert the Maoris. Dissension and fighting were the results, although it was possession of the land that contributed mostly to hostilities between Maori and Pakeha and even brought about intertribal divisions. In an effort to secure peace between the Maoris and the English, the English government negotiated a treaty with the Maoris, the Treaty of Waitangi (Wuh-ee-tuh-ngee) on February 6, 1840. This agreement represents the beginning of a new chapter in the history of modern New Zealand, a history that is now being written by a united people.

New Zealand Cities

Communities with a population of more than 20,000 people are given city status. There are over twenty-three such cities in New Zealand today. The four main cities of Auckland, Wellington, Christchurch, and Dunedin are evenly spaced down the length of the country. Each has a good port and is an industrial center.

16

Auckland functions as a seaport and airport, serving the rich Waikato (Wuh-ee-kuh-taw) and Northland dairying districts, and is a leading industrial center and one of the country's fastest growing cities. Since this area enjoys a subtropical climate, the main harbor, Waitemata (Wuh-ee-te-muh-tuh), serves more yachts and pleasure craft than any other city of its size in the world. Auckland handles a large import tonnage. The city also has the country's largest university. The main area of Auckland is connected to a fast-growing residential section north of the city by a harbor bridge over two-thirds of a mile long. An international airport provides overseas jet services.

Wellington, the capital of New Zealand, is at the southern tip of North Island in the geographical center of the country. In this city are located the buildings of Parliament, the head office of all Ministries, many national organizations, banks, commercial firms, and Victoria University of Wellington. The city has a large and attractive natural harbor surrounded by steep hills. The city of Wellington itself has little room for expansion, and many of its workers live in rapidly growing "satellite" areas.

Left: Aerial view of Auckland showing North Shore, Devonport, and looking up Waitemata Harbor to the Harbor Bridge. Auckland is New Zealand's largest city.

Right: Buildings of Canterbury University in Christchurch, South Island's largest city.

17

Christchurch, near the middle of the east coast of South Island, is the center of the great lamb, wool, and grain province of Canterbury. Its parks, avenues, street lanes, beautiful rose gardens, and imposing cathedral mark Christchurch as the most characteristically English of New Zealand cities. The port of Christchurch is separated from the city by hills but is connected by road and rail tunnels. This city is also known for Lincoln College, an internationally famous center of agricultural learning and research, and Canterbury University which features an important industrial development program.

Dunedin, the second largest city in South Island, is 230 miles south of Christchurch. This city has strong links with Edinburgh, Scotland, whose ancient Scottish name it bears. Dunedin was once the most prosperous city in New Zealand after the discovery of gold in 1861, and for about a generation the city had financial pros-

18

Left: Wellington, city and harbor, becomes a brilliant scene at night with lights mirrored in Oriental Bay and viewed against the dramatic backdrop of Mount Victoria. Daytime reveals a city that reminds Americans of San Francisco.

The central government was first located at Auckland. Wellington became the capital after 1865.

Right: First Church of Otago in Dunedin, a city renowned for its Scottish charm.

perity. But as the supply of gold dwindled, so did Dunedin's prosperity. At present, with the movement of many of its young people to the north, Dunedin has the lowest annual rate of increase of all New Zealand cities. Dunedin's university, the University of Otago, is held in high repute.

One of the most popular hot springs resort areas in New Zealand is Rotorua (Raw-taw-roo-uh) on North Island. Originally a Maori settlement, many descendants of the native people live there. Rotorua is located in a volcanic plateau where some of the volcanoes are still active. The land is dotted with geysers and boiling pools of mud and water. South of Rotorua at Wairakei (Wuh-ee-*raa*-keh-ee), underground steam is harnessed to produce electricity. At one time, the natural hot springs were utilized by the Maoris for cooking.

19

New Zealand's Parliament in session. Parliament is made up of the legislative council (the upper house) and the house of representatives (the lower house).

New Zealand's Government

New Zealand is an independent, self-governing member of the British Commonwealth of Nations. This means that New Zealanders make their own decisions in the operation of their government, but they are still loyal to their mother country, England. Thus, the British queen is also the queen of New Zealand. The reigning monarch, Queen Elizabeth II, is represented in New Zealand by a Governor-General who is appointed by the Queen and serves for a period of five years.

The political system is democratic and is modeled on that of Great Britain. There is a Parliament elected by men and women who are at least twenty years of age. It is interesting that New Zealand was the last major area of the world to be settled by the white man, but it was the first country to give the vote to women. This was done in 1893.

Government policy is established by legislation, and the party in power is represented by the prime minister who appoints cabinet ministers to head each of the government departments. The party in power is known as the "government." The major party out of

power is known as the "opposition." The opposition tries to oppose the government when it thinks an unwise decision has been made, thus serving as a check on the power of the decision makers.

In 1962, following the example of Sweden, the New Zealand government appointed an *ombudsman* (om-*budz*-mun) to investigate the complaints of citizens against actions of the state administration or the government. Experience has shown that the ombudsman serves a useful purpose in correcting situations disagreeable to the people.

A modern hydroelectric plant harnesses the energy of the natural geysers.

Below: A Prime Minister of New Zealand opens a meeting of the Economic Commission for Asia and the Far East.

New Zealand's Public Services

Private enterprise predominates in business, but essential services such as railways, airlines, postal and telegraph services, electricity, and radio and television broadcasting all come under public ownership, that is, government ownership. Nearly all of New Zealand's shipping is privately owned.

New Zealand's International Relations

New Zealand, although geographically small and isolated, is deeply involved in world affairs and plays an active role in the community of free nations.

As a country of predominately British origin, it has close links with Britain. New Zealand is allied with its nearest neighbor, Australia, and with the United States under the ANZUS (Australia-New Zealand-United States) Treaty which links these three nations together.

New Zealand is a founding member of the South-East Asia Treaty Organization (SEATO) and the United Nations Organization.

New Zealand's defense policy is based on the principle of collective security since New Zealand realizes that it is not able to defend its own isolated strategic area alone. Nevertheless, this staunch little nation has participated vigorously in working with other member nations with interest in the South Pacific.

Left: Merino are considered a fine-wool sheep. In this scene at Glentanner Station, Canterbury, wool is being clipped from around the eyes of the animals.

Right: Sheep Mustering, Marlborough Province, South Island. The mule team pushes ahead of the sheep to set up camp.

New Zealand's Resources

Although New Zealand appears to be rich in mineral resources, few significant deposits have been found. Bituminous and brown coal are mined in both North and South Islands in the country's many coal mines. This coal is used for domestic needs such as industrial use, electricity, briquettes, and a small amount is used for railroads and gas production.

Gold mining boomed in the 1860s and contributed greatly to the early progress and settlement of New Zealand, then declined in importance.

A significant increase in exportation in recent years reflects the growing interest in the potential resources of New Zealand. Dairy products continue to be major exports, but a marked expansion in manufacturing is taking place. New Zealand's ability to effectively use its resources is demonstrated by the fact that before World War II, New Zealand maintained the highest overseas trade in proportion to population of any country in the world, a position attained in a brief 100 years.

24

New Zealand's Agriculture and Industry

New Zealand is one of the leading farming countries in the world, despite the fact that it does not have naturally fertile land. The volcanic soil has required fertilization, and the development of rich grasslands has been due to expert pasture management and farm research. Since cattle and sheep can be raised in the pastures all year round and the climate is among the best in the world, farming has become the most important occupation in New Zealand.

The farms of New Zealand carry more than sixty-million sheep and over eight-million cattle. A high percent of export earnings come from the sale of farm products such as meat, wool, butter, and cheese. The development of highly efficient grassland farming has enabled New Zealand to become the biggest commercial exporter of meat and dairy products in the world and the second largest exporter of wool.

Most of the large sheep farms of the pioneering days have now been divided, and flocks have become smaller, averaging about 1,000 sheep. In recent years, New Zealand has supplied much of the frozen mutton and frozen lamb imported into Britain. Increasing quantities of mutton are now being exported elsewhere, with some going to Japan.

As a result of extensive promotion work, there is a continuing demand overseas for New Zealand beef. To help meet this demand, New Zealand farmers are systematically increasing beef cattle herds. The most popular beef breed is the Aberdeen Angus, with the Hereford and Shorthorn next in number. Four-fifths of the dairy cows are Jerseys.

All butter and cheese factories and all but two of the dried-milk factories are owned by the farmers of the districts they serve. Co-operative enterprise has characterized the dairy industry for many years. Refrigerated stainless steel tankers transport the milk from the farms to the factories. Most of the dairy factory plants and machinery are made in New Zealand.

Through the systematic application of the most modern methods of processing, New Zealand's dairy and meat products have won a high international reputation for consistent quality. The special importance attached to hygiene is the main reason for this caliber of production.

All overseas marketing of dairy products is done by the New Zealand Dairy Board, an organization of producer and government representatives. To suit the British taste, New Zealand has developed a salted butter distinguished by a gold color. This butter is now established in many export markets as well. The cheese exported is mainly a rich Cheddar. A wide variety of other cheeses has been produced in recent years; one in particular, a Roquefort-type cheese, has been a popular export.

Apples and pears are exported in large quantities, mainly to Britain and Europe. Apricots and strawberries are flown into British and European markets during the northern winter (December to February).

26

Above Left: Pedigree Polled Hereford cattle on a farm at Portland near Whangarei, North Island. Whangarei Harbor is in the distance. New Zealand provides good grazing for beef cattle.

Right: A young New Zealander enjoys some of the luscious peaches from orchards in sunny Hawke's Bay Province of North Island.

Packing apples, Mapua, Auckland Province in North Island.

New Zealand exports large quantities of forest products. At the Tasman Pulp and Paper Mill, Kawerau, a giant hammerhead crane unloads a thirty-ton wagonload of logs in one lift.

The melter is a worker in charge of the melting and purifying of scrap iron in the production of steel. Here, the melter on the forty-ton electric arc furnace at Pacific Steel, Ltd, Auckland, charges limestone to make the slag necessary to remove impurities from the liquid steel. He wears dark glasses against the intense glare of the furnace.

Of special interest is the growing forestry industry. Over 40,000 people are employed, and expansion of the industry will both reduce New Zealand's imports of timber and wood products and increase foreign exchange earnings. Tauranga (*Tuh-oo*-ruh-nguh) has become an important port for the exportation of logs from New Zealand's forests.

The pulp and paper industry, based upon planted forests, began about thirty years ago. Major expansion took place in the mid-1950s with the opening of two large factories, and there has been significant development in both increasing and diversifying production. Australia offers the biggest market, but exportation to Japan is steadily increasing.

Commercial development of any great significance for the fishing industry lies in the future, as fishing is primarily regarded as a sport. Crayfishing is a major industry, but New Zealand has joined with conservationists around the world in the preservation of crayfish and forms of sea life.

Hydroelectric resources are making possible the development of aluminum and steel production. At the same time, there is an ever-increasing concern for conservation of the environment.

Left: The Waitomo Glow-worm Cave in North Island is one of the most beautiful sights found in New Zealand. Hundreds of thousands of glowworms cover the walls and roof of a giant cavern. The soft blue-green light given off by the insects illuminates the chamber and produces an unusual effect.

Right: Beach scene at Te Kaha, Bay of Plenty, North Island. Alluring beaches dot the coastline of New Zealand.

New Zealand—A Traveler's Delight

New Zealand attracts people from all over the world because of its beauty and unusual attractions.

North Island has lush pasture land, forests, and the exciting phenomenon of thermal activity, as well as the interesting Maori culture. The Glowworm Grotto at Waitomo (*Wuh-ee*-taw-maw) Caves is often described as one of the wonders of the world. Rotorua has spectacular geysers, hot springs, and bubbling mud pools. Lakes and trout fishing, along with the three mountains of Tongariro National Park, one of them a large, active volcano, are some of the highlights of North Island.

Continuing to South Island, the visitor is impressed with the dramatic impact of the Southern Alps, a scene dominated by majestic Mount Cook. Mountains, forests, and lakes vie for attention with the two great glaciers which descend almost to the sea from the snows of the Southern Alps.

Sports are also a great incentive for visitors. Within easy reach of all cities are lakes, mountains, rivers, and beaches. Most New Zealanders enjoy sports such as rowing, swimming, mountain climbing, walking, cycling, skiing, boating, shooting, and deep sea fishing.

The most popular winter sport is rugby, and the New Zealand team is called the "All Blacks" because the fifteen players wear black shorts, jerseys, and socks. This team is recognized as one of the strongest rugby teams in the world.

Both freshwater and big game fishing are very rewarding in New Zealand. Rainbow and brown trout averaging three to four pounds are popular freshwater catches, while game fishing includes kingfish; swordfish; marlin; mako, thresher, and hammerhead shark; albacore; and tuna.

Left: Hotel-to-Glacier delivery service. Climbers arrive at the snowfields, fresh and fully equiped for their sport. On its flight the ski-plane passes between jagged snow-covered peaks, giving passengers an unparalleled view of the Southern Alps.

Right: Mount Cook, the highest peak of the Southern Alps, as viewed from above Hooker Glacier.

Left: A general view of Maraetai powerhouse and dam.

Right: Pine trees in the Waihura cutting section of approximately 1700 acres located in the Kaingaroa forest near Rotorua.

Girls of the Brigadiers team, Auckland, with eyes right salute in march past.

An aerial view of Mangere International Airport, Auckland, New Zealand.

New Zealand Today—and Tomorrow

By international standards New Zealanders live well. New Zealand's average standard of living places it among the top six countries of the world.

Most New Zealand workers have a basic forty-hour, five-day week. All employees, including farm workers, are guaranteed by law a two-week paid vacation yearly in addition to national holidays. Although taxes are high in New Zealand, tax revenue provides hospital and medical care for citizens; cash benefits for the aged, the blind, and others permanently incapacitated for work; and for widows, orphans, the unemployed, and wage workers unable to work because of sickness or accident. The government pays varying

35

Tasman Glacier from Ball Pass, Mount Cook National Park. This scene typifies New Zealander's view of the future of their land—bright and optimistic.

amounts toward the costs of medical attention. Nearly all the medicine prescribed by doctors is free to patients. The government also meets hospital expenses and contributes toward the expenses of patients in private hospitals. Government-provided infant-care services have helped to reduce New Zealand's mortality rate to one of the lowest in the world.

Free public education is also available up to the age of nineteen and compulsory to the age of fifteen. Children three to five years of age may attend free play centers and free kindergartens. An unusual feature of the Department of Education is a correspondence school with teachers providing instruction by mail for over 5,000 pupils in isolated areas, in other Pacific islands, in hospitals, and in prisons.

New Zealanders are rightfully proud of the many advantages which they enjoy. Despite the limited area with which they have had to work and the lateness of their settlement, the people of New Zealand have created a way of life that commands respect throughout the world community. They are proud to be a part of New Zealand today.